Theological Education in Asia

Theological Education in Asia

Discipleship and Suffering

JOHAN FERREIRA

WIPF & STOCK · Eugene, Oregon

THEOLOGICAL EDUCATION IN ASIA
Discipleship and Suffering

Wipf & Stock
An Imprint of Wipf and Stock Publishers
199 W. 8th Ave., Suite 3
Eugene, OR 97401

www.wipfandstock.com

PAPERBACK ISBN: 978-1-7252-7781-6
HARDCOVER ISBN: 978-1-7252-7782-3
EBOOK ISBN: 978-1-7252-7783-0

Manufactured in the U.S.A.   09/18/20

Contents

Preface

CHRISTIANITY HAS GROWN EXPONENTIALLY in Asia over the last
hundred years, especially during the last few decades. A century
ago, approximately only 1 percent of Asians were Christian; today,
the figure is close to 7 percent. With this amazing development of
Christianity in Asia, many theological colleges have sprung up in
the last thirty years to meet the urgent need to train pastors and
Christian leaders.

Theological education is one of the most critical enterprises
for the church and for Asia today. The future witness of Christianity
in Asia, the work of pastors and Christian leaders, and the success
of Christian mission are directly related to the quality of theological education. Churches reflect their pastors, and pastors in turn
reflect their theological colleges. Unfortunately, many theological
colleges in Asia (and the world) are less than ideal. There is a lack
of resources, and colleges often operate in contexts that are antago-
nistic towards the Christian faith. However, perhaps the greatest
challenge does not lie in external constraints, but in the internal
cultural and educational processes of the colleges themselves.
Educational programs often lack focus and do not produce the in-
tended outcomes, which can be seen in the lives and ministries of
graduates. It is my firm belief that the lack of a sound theology of
theological education is one of the contributing factors behind the
weaknesses that we observe in colleges and churches today. Many
churches and pastors need to rediscover the gospel and what it
means to be true disciples of Jesus in today's world. In other words,

there is an urgent need for theological educators to recognize the fundamental importance of a theology of theological education and to implement such a theology in their educational institutions. Therefore, the purpose of this monograph is to present a theology of theological education for debate and reflection.

This monograph consists of three parts. The first part, by way of introduction, briefly considers the challenges that theological education in Asia faces today. The second part of the study considers the Great Commission in Matthew 28:18–20 as the basis for a theology of theological education. Theological education essentially fulfils the purpose of the Great Commission, which concerns discipleship. The third part of the study considers the key text on discipleship in Matthew 16:24, asserting that suffering is an essential aspect of following Jesus. The study argues that discipleship and a theology of suffering must feature prominently in theological education. There are also three appendices that may be useful for theological educators: a set of Graduate Attributes, a code of Professional Ethics for Ministers, and a statement on Spiritual Abuse.[1]

1. An earlier version of the second part of this study appeared in Ferreira, "Great Commission."

Challenges in Theological Education

DUE TO THE RAPID growth of Christianity in Asia and the pressing need to train more pastors and teachers for the church, many theological colleges have been established in the last three decades. For example, Yangon, the capital of Myanmar, has more than a hundred colleges or centers that offer theological training. While some colleges are based on the traditional models in the West and others are newer and employ innovative approaches, they all face significant pressure to adapt to a fast-changing society. Also, with the rise of educational standards in Asia and increasing globalization, there is a great desire among Asian Christians for formal theological qualifications.

All these factors contribute to significant changes in theological education, from the more traditional approaches to a plethora of new innovations and "market-driven" programs. These changes inevitably raise questions: What can be said about how we have traditionally practiced theological education? What can be said about the theological foundation of these newer approaches? Is theological education advancing or regressing in Asia? It appears that although there are many new approaches, there is little theological reflection on the legitimacy of these approaches. This is regrettable. Few evangelical Christians will disagree that it is essential for theological education, more so than for other spheres of activity, to be grounded upon a sound biblical theology. It is therefore necessary, especially for those who are involved in this most important enterprise, to reflect on the theology of theological education.[1]

In order to have a clearer picture of the challenge before us, we need to consider the state of theological education in Asia as a whole, which is in fact not hugely different from the rest of the world. Theological education is currently being challenged in several ways. Although there are regional variations, there are questions about the legitimacy of the enterprise, pressing economic constraints, as well as the influence of pragmatic consumerism. In some countries, there is great antagonism, if not open persecution, towards the Christian faith, which make it very difficult for theological colleges to operate.[2] In other countries, there have been a decline in faculty numbers at some theological institutions due to the increasing costs of education and budgetary constraints. The third and potentially more challenging threat is consumerism or pragmatism. Globally, education has become very pragmatic and empirically orientated. Since the philosophy of pragmatism rejects the concept of ultimate reality, the task of education is not to pass on bodies of knowledge, which is seen as irrelevant, but to prepare students for the "real" world by developing employable skills for the marketplace. Education is not to be teacher- or subject-centered, but student-centered.[3] It is activity-based and

---

1. I echo the same sentiments as Robert Banks: " . . . in the debate so far there has been little reflection on what the Bible might contribute to our understanding of theological education." Banks, *Reenvisioning Theological Education*, 73.

2. Noelliste, "Handmaiden to God's Economy," 15.

3. With respect to teaching, the Bible does emphasize the experience and context of the student, but at the same time, it does not ignore the value of factual knowledge or rote learning. Note Judith and Sherwood Lingenfelter: "Modern educators have commonly rejected imitation and rote learning techniques. They have argued that these strategies limit creativity and innovative learning. Yet Scripture teaches us that these techniques have been employed for thousands of years to enrich one's life in community and walk with God." Lingenfelter, *Teaching Cross-Culturally*, 39. Recent studies have shown that rote learning is not incompatible with higher orders of thinking but in fact may enhance creativity. See Watkins and Biggs, *Chinese Learner*.

problem-orientated.[4] This *Zeitgeist* is also making its presence felt in theological education in Asia with the increasing emphasis on vocational training and the marketplace. While it is important to develop the necessary practical skills for ministry, this overtly empirical model of education is inherently flawed and unbiblical. Together with the great desire for official qualifications among Asian Christians, these challenges have led to lowered standards in some places.

In general, theological education or theological institutions can be divided into two paradigms; namely, a radical/liberal paradigm and a conservative/evangelical paradigm. Although there are a variety of styles within each of these paradigms, this general demarcation holds true. Liberal theological institutions are facing a crisis. If current trends continue, many of these institutions will contract or even close down over the next few years. However, conservative institutions, while facing some challenges, are doing well. What is the reason behind this different state of affairs? One reason for the decline of liberal theological institutions, which also contains an important lesson for those in evangelical colleges, is that these institutions have moved away from their traditional roots or from the mission of the church. Theological education cannot be divorced from the mission of the church. The relationship between the church and the theological institution is the umbilical cord that not only validates but also sustains theological education. The crisis that we find in traditional theological institutions is by and large due to a severing of this umbilical cord. Medical training exists for the hospital; so too, theological education exists for the service of the church. Once the mission of the church fades away from the primary focus of theological education, decline is the inevitable result.

4. For a discussion of various educational philosophies from a Christian perspective see Peterson, *Philosophy of Education*. Peterson states, "With its emphasis on technology and satisfactory consequences, experimentalism expresses the mood of contemporary American and Western European life." Peterson, *Philosophy of Education*, 59. This pragmatic orientation is also reflected in the current insistence on outcomes assessment. See Aleshire, "Character and Assessment of Learning for Religious Vocation."

When we observe conservative or evangelical theological institutions, there is a different picture. There is a continuing and even increasing demand from evangelical Christians for theological education. Naturally, these Christians generally seek to study at evangelical institutions rather than the more liberal ones. Evangelical institutions want to maintain the beliefs and convictions of historic Christianity and see themselves as serving the churches. In other words, there continues to be a strong link with the mission of the church.

However, with the increasing demand for theological education there has also been a great proliferation of theological institutions and programs, often with a very practical orientation. These programs provide a service to the members of the local constituency, but they tend to undermine the viability of the more established theological colleges as student numbers are spread more thinly.[5] In Asia, many Western institutions are also now offering intensives and online courses which are easily accessible. These Western institutions are seeking to export their "product" in order to increase their "market" and influence. This increased competition tends to undermine local institutions and is forcing many colleges to reassess and adjust their programs to suit the marketplace, which can be both good and bad. While theological institutions must be in-step with the needs of both church and society, there is a danger of being driven solely by pragmatics that may in fact undermine the theology and beliefs that the institution is supposed to propagate. The competition between theological colleges for the limited pool of students may also cultivate a worldly mindset and non-Christian behavior.

---

5. With fewer students and less revenue, faculty numbers and the quality of resources will decline. Eventually, this will cause a problem not only for the provision of high-quality degrees, but especially for the provision of higher theological degrees. There are very few colleges in Asia with an evangelical *ethos* that can provide quality theological research degrees. It appears that in the future, the only option for many evangelicals wishing to pursue research degrees will be either at liberal and sparsely resourced university departments or overseas.

Theological education in Asia is facing significant challenges. How should we respond? For Christians, there can only be one adequate response, which is to return to the Bible and reassess the basis and purpose of theological education. Our views and practices must be based on a sound biblical theology of theological education.

Towards a Theology
of Theological Education

PRELIMINARY OBSERVATIONS

THE PURPOSE OF THIS study is to reflect briefly on theological education in light of the above-mentioned circumstances, and to propose a simple but practical and biblical theology of theological education. At the outset, however, some preliminary comments are in order. A theology of theological education lies in the area of practical theology, which is not an exact science. In other words, as with other areas in practical theology, in the end we will need to be content with an approximation of the ideal. We may be confident, as far as our abilities allow, to construct a sound theology or ideal model of theological education, but compromise is inevitable when we enter the real world and attempt to implement that model. We are always going to live somewhere between "the now and the not yet" or "the ideal and the reality." However, that should not deter us from aiming for what is more perfect.

For Christians, the starting point of reflection should be the Bible.[1] Indeed, as I reflected on the topic, I became more and more convinced that the best place to start looking for a theology of theological education is the Great Commission. The enterprise of theological education is in fact a central aspect of the outworking

1. Scripture is the Word of God and the yardstick for theology and *practice*. Since God's revelation is culture-directed, rather than culturally conditioned, Scriptural models must be taken seriously. Form and meaning are intrinsically related. See Kossen, "Interpreting and Applying Scripture."

of the commission that Jesus gave the disciples in Matt 28:18–20. This study therefore proposes that the foundation of theological education is found in the Great Commission. The Great Commission crystallizes the great themes in the Gospel of Matthew, not the least of which is mission. The Great Commission forms the grand overview of Jesus' plan. It is a paradigmatic statement that should govern the ministry and intentions of the disciples. In particular, the Great Commission provides the justification (why?), the content (what?), as well as the methodology (how?), not just of mission, but also of theological education. This study will consider these three aspects as they relate to theological education.[2] In Matt 28:18–20, we read as follows:

> And Jesus came and said to them, "All authority in heaven and on earth has been given to me. Go therefore and make disciples of all nations, baptizing them in the name of the Father and of the Son and of the Holy Spirit, teaching them to observe all that I have commanded you. And behold, I am with you always, to the end of the age."

THE "WHY" OF THEOLOGICAL EDUCATION

Why do we spend so much time and effort on theological education? How can we justify, and on some occasions defend, theological education? Should it be done? Why can't we do without it? Jesus' first words to his disciples in the Great Commission provide the basis and rationale for mission, and as we will see, also for theological education. "All authority has been given to me in heaven and on earth." As the result of his redemptive work on the cross and his victorious resurrection from the dead, Jesus received or "was given" all authority. The aorist passive verb *edothē* [ἐδόθη] states the fact of the

---

2. Also see "ICAA Manifesto on the Renewal of Evangelical Theological Education." It addresses twelve areas for renewal: (1) contextualization; (2) churchward orientation; (3) strategic flexibility; (4) theological grounding; (5) continuous assessment; (6) community life; (7) integrated program; (8) servant moulding; (9) instructional variety; (10) a Christian mind; (11) equipping for growth; and (12) cooperation.

conferral of authority upon Jesus. The passive voice of the verb can be interpreted as a theological passive; i.e., God the Father is the agent of the action. The Father did not abandon Jesus on the cross but vindicated him through the resurrection and has now bestowed all "authority" upon him. Jesus has therefore been "authorized" to continue his mission in the world. The word "authority" [ἐξουσία: *exousia*] implies both the right to act and the ability to act,[3] and with the "therefore" [οὖν: *oun*] of verse 19, Jesus shows that he is indeed prepared to act on this authority.

Furthermore, it is important to note that Jesus is now Lord not only in heaven, but also on the earth. Before the cross, the devil wielded power on earth (Matt 4:8–9), but now it has been handed over to Jesus. He is the eschatological figure proclaimed in Dan 7:13–14 who will inaugurate the kingdom of God on earth and whom all people will serve and worship.[4] Jesus is the universal king to whom all honor is due. What was intimated in Matthew 2 with the coming and worship of the wise men from the East is now fully realized. The kingdom of heaven has broken into the world and must now be proclaimed to all nations. It is on this basis that Christians believe they have the authority, and indeed, the obligation, to extend the kingdom throughout the world and into all areas of life and culture. In the words of Bruner:

> Christians are now hopelessly, incurably missionary and evangelistic, no matter how people tell them of the need for the church's conversion to the world or of the end of mission or of the danger of missions to national and ethnic treasures.[5]

The mission of realizing the kingdom of heaven on earth must continue.

Likewise, it is the commission of the risen Lord that provides the presupposition and justification of theological education. This is the indispensable context of theological education. In view of

---

3. cf. Matt 7:29; 8:9; 20:25; 21:23, 24, 27.

4. The wording of the Septuagint of Dan 7:14 is similar to the language of the Great Commission.

5. Bruner, *Matthew*, 1098.

the authority and commission of the Lord, we must engage in the enterprise of theological education. It is a matter of obedience and of worship. In Matt 28:17, when the disciples saw Jesus, they "worshipped him." These convictions and attitudes should pervade the exercise of theological education. It is at the feet of the crucified and risen Lord, in humble adoration and thankfulness, where we should conduct the study of theology.[6] As in Jewish thought, worship and the study of the Scriptures are one and the same thing. Again, here we have the very lifeblood of theological education. Once theological education divorces itself from the mission of the church and the worship of the Lord, it becomes like the branch that leaves the vine and withers. Theological education must engage itself with the crucified and risen Lord in obedient service and worship. The proper sphere of theological education is not the university but the church, not academia but mission. It is crucial that teachers of theology understand this fundamental difference between the university and the theological college.[7]

THE "WHAT" OF THEOLOGICAL EDUCATION

Having provided a theological justification for theological education, we may turn to matters of curriculum. What should be taught? What should be the focus of the teaching and learning? The content of theological education has always been a matter of debate. The Great Commission can be very instructive, and indeed should be determinative, as we reflect on this question. When we look at the commission itself, it is important to note that strictly speaking, there is only one command or imperative, and that is "to make disciples" [μαθητεύσατε: *mathēteusate*]. The imperative

6. Note Warfield's comments on the study of theology, "In all its branches alike, theology has as its unique end to make God known: the student of theology is brought by his daily task into the presence of God and is kept there. Can a religious man stand in the presence of God and not worship?" Warfield, "Religious Life of Theological Students," 34.

7. So too, Foord notes, "It is a terrible mistake to use teachers whose desire is simply to do academic theology without reference to real-life ministry." Foord, "Elements of a Theology of Theological Education," 41.

is qualified with three participles (go, baptize, teach), which are subject to the main verb (i.e., the imperative). Therefore, the focal point of the commission, both syntactically and theologically, lies in the imperative. A consideration of the meaning of the imperative is highly informative for understanding mission in general and theological education in particular. The verb *mathēteuō* [μαθητεύω], used transitively here, means "to make disciples of," "to make students of," or "to educate" someone. According to Bruner, it refers to "an educational process more than an evangelistic crisis, a school more than a revival."[8] Consequently, the aim of making disciples involves a pedagogical process rather than merely obtaining decisions or commitments. The Great Commission at its heart speaks about theological education. It is then appropriate to see the foundation of theological education in the Great Commission.

But what must be the focus of this education? As stated above, the main verb (the imperative) basically means "to educate." But to what end? Clearly, it means to educate people ("all nations") in order for them to become disciples of the Lord. Therefore, the main goal of theological education must be discipleship; that is, the following of the Lord. Christopher Duraisingh also emphasizes the importance of mission in theological education:

> In sum, our philosophy of theological education influences the kind of curriculum we adopt. The purpose of theological education is not the training in abstract theological thought for respectable scholarship, but to enable the Church to fulfil her mission in the world.[9]

So too, Lee Wanak comments:

> . . . theological education is to be missional, in tune with the *missio Dei*, fleshing out the Gospel of the kingdom of God and equipping people to live as citizens and soldiers of that kingdom. When missional focus is lost,

---

8. Bruner, *Matthew,* 1096.

9. Duraisingh, "Ministerial Formation for Mission," 149.

theological education is reduced to an academic exercise and God-talk.[10]

Therefore, becoming passionate disciples of Jesus must be one of the major goals and outcomes of theological education.[11]

Accordingly, it is important to stress that discipleship implies the following of a person, rather than merely gaining understanding of a system of knowledge. In Matt 10:24–25, Jesus says, "A disciple is not above his teacher, nor a servant above his master." This key statement in the Gospel of Matthew captures an essential characteristic of discipleship.[12] The goal of the disciple is to become *like* the master. Here we have a unique difference between theological education and other forms of education. A student is different from a disciple. A student of Marx is not necessarily a follower of Marx. But a disciple is both a student and a follower. Christian discipleship goes a step further—it is becoming like the Lord. The purpose of educational systems today is for students to develop skills in order to gain employment.[13] Personal development—matters of character—does not receive much emphasis. However, the goal of theological education, in the perspective of the Great Commission, should be to develop disciples. Character formation is all-important. This *imitatio Christi* principle must lie at the heart of theological education to fulfill its goal. It is about transforming ordinary people into the likeness of Christ.[14]

10. Deininger and Eguizabal, "Developing an Operational Philosophy of Theological Education," 44.

11. In the example of Graduate Attributes in Appendix 1, passionate discipleship is listed as the first aim of theological education.

12. Also see Luke 6:40.

13. Sometimes, theological education is also viewed in this light. Churches are more interested in what the pastor can do than in what the pastor understands or who the pastor is.

14. Commenting on the importance of transformation in theological education David McEwan states, "Conceptually, this speaks to us of the primacy of character and that the goal of our education process is the transformation of the person into the image of Christ, not merely to acquire knowledge via effective data transmission." McEwan, "Quality Theological Education," 101.

This principle has wide-ranging implications for theological education.[15] We will make only a few comments here. The *imitatio Christi* principle implies that theological education must be holistic. The disciple is concerned to follow the full Christ, involving aspects of "head, hand, and heart." Students need to have the right knowledge, the right skills, and the right character (i.e., personal qualities) to be effective in ministry. However, in view of the meaning of discipleship, "the heart"—or spiritual formation—is central. Yet in today's theological institution, this aspect is probably the least emphasized.[16] Being a disciple is, above all, being a witness *of* the Lord, not just *to* the Lord. In practice, this would mean that much time is to be spent facilitating spiritual growth and maturity. Spiritual formation should be intentional and at the core of the curriculum.[17] This could perhaps be achieved through integrating aspects of spiritual formation with the usual subject areas, and also more emphasis on the spiritual disciplines within the program.[18] In fact, this biblical emphasis on spiritual formation sits very well with

15. For example, in my own area of biblical studies, one cannot confine the discussion only to the "original meaning" of the text; more importantly, one must allow the text to reshape or transform identity and practice. See Melugin, "Texts to Transform Life."

16. One reason for this neglect is no doubt the difficulty of implementing effective spiritual formation within an academic program. Note Judith and Sherwood Lingenfelter's comment, "Teaching for transformation of character and ministry is the most difficult of all teaching challenges. Seminaries, colleges, and secondary schools excel in the transmission of information, but few take responsibility for the character and performance of their graduates. Most recognize the critical need for character and spiritual formation, but few have found effective ways to achieve these objectives." Lingenfelter, *Teaching Cross-Culturally*, 96.

17. Note that in the example of Graduate Attributes in Appendix 1, the third outcome specially deals with issues of character.

18. There needs to be much more emphasis on the spiritual disciplines. "Christian discipline and mutual accountability, prayer and fasting, watching, self-denial, taking up one's cross, love feasts, covenant services, the Eucharist, searching the Scriptures, tradition, prayers, and hymns. Students must not be told about these as academic curiosities, but must be immersed in them, so that they in turn can replicate the means in the communities of faith they will serve." McEwan, "Quality Theological Education," 106.

Chinese educational philosophy. Traditional Chinese education has stressed the centrality of the cultivation of the person, which is achieved through learning and vigorous conduct. In *The Great Learning*, the classical treatise on education, personal formation is especially prominent: "From the Son of Heaven down to the mass of the people, all must consider the cultivation of the person the root of every thing besides."[19]

The importance of the *imitatio Christi* principle is again emphasized in the third participial clause of the commission; they must make disciples by "teaching them to observe all that I have commanded you." For this to happen, the disciple needs to be instructed in the life and teachings of the Lord. According to the context, and for the original readers of Matthew, those commandments are contained in the Gospel of Matthew. In other words, the central focus of theological education should be spiritual formation through the study of the life and teachings of Jesus in the Gospels. According to Martin Foord, "An evangelical understanding of theological education must begin with the gospel itself (evangeliology)."[20] This is more or less stating the obvious. The Gospels are the center of the Scriptures and lie at the heart of Christian faith and practice. We study the Old Testament because it leads into the Gospels by providing the context. We study the rest of the New Testament, theology, church history, and practical theology, because they proceed out of the Gospels. Although it is necessary, even indispensable, to study Old Testament, theology, church history, and practical theology, the ultimate goal of theological education is to become followers of the Lord and to become like the Lord. This is also what the Apostle Paul refers to when he says, "And we all, with unveiled face, beholding the glory of the Lord, are being transformed into the same image from one degree of glory to another. For this comes from the Lord who is the Spirit" (2 Cor 3:18). Therefore, I propose that the study of the Gospels, for the purpose of becoming followers of the Lord and of being

19. Legge, *Chinese Classics*, 223.
20. Foord, "Elements of a Theology of Theological Education," 41.

transformed into his image, should be the unifying center of the theological curriculum.[21]

THE "HOW" OF THEOLOGICAL EDUCATION

Methodology, or the "how" question, is probably the most debated issue in theological education today. A multitude of models have been suggested. David H. Kelsey, professor of theology at Yale University, identifies two basic models in the history of Western theological education: the Athens model and the Berlin model.[22] The Athens model, prevalent during the Medieval Ages, developed out of the context of Greek culture and emphasized the formation of character. The Berlin model is based on the German university and regards theology as a scientific discipline with its own system of knowledge that is to be mastered by the student. This latter approach places much emphasis on intellectual development.[23] On the basis of Kelsey's analysis, Robert Banks suggests a new model—the Jerusalem model.[24] This model combines the Athens and Berlin approaches, but more importantly, it emphasizes mission *praxis*. In this model, much ministry formation occurs in the church rather than in the classroom. Banks argues that this model is more authentic to the New Testament. Finally, on the basis of these studies, Brian Edgar proposed four models of theological education: the Athens model (classical), the Geneva model (confessional), the Berlin (academic), and the Jerusalem (missional).[25]

---

21. We may also note in the example of Graduate Attributes in Appendix 1 that the third outcome specially deals with issues of character.

22. Kelsey, *To Understand God Truly*.

23. This academic approach is reflected by Warfield, "The importance of the intellectual preparation of the student for the ministry is the reason of the existence of our Theological Seminaries. Say what you will, do what you will, the ministry is a 'learned profession'; and the man without learning, no matter with what other gifts he may be endowed, is unfit for its duties." Warfield, "Religious Life of Theological Students," 31.

24. Banks, *Reenvisioning Theological Education*.

25. Edgar, "Theology of Theological Education."

In light of this historical background, which is the best road for theological colleges in Asia to take?

Certainly, the most prevalent model over the last hundred years in the West has been the academic or university model. In the last few decades, the vocational model has come to the fore. Instead of focusing on knowledge, the vocational model focuses on transferring specific ministry skills to students. The purpose of theological education here is to prepare the student for the demands of employment.[26] All these approaches have strengths, but also weaknesses. Is there another alternative? The Great Commission also guides us in how to conduct theological education; it integrates the best aspects of all four approaches as outlined by Brian Edgar into a coherent whole.

When we look at the Great Commission, a beautiful and well-reasoned structure appears. As mentioned above, the main verb "to make disciples" is qualified by three subordinate participial clauses. These clauses inform us how the imperative is to be fulfilled; that is, through *going, baptizing,* and *teaching.*[27] The following diagram illustrates the relationship between the main verb "to make disciples" and the three subordinating participles: going, baptizing, and teaching.

26. This vocational approach is reflected by Jung Sung Rhee, "Here we find differences in structures among our three countries (Japan, Taiwan and Korea), but there is no difference in the purpose of theological education, which is to train men and women for church work either as pastors or evangelists. For this reason all courses at seminaries are structured in order to train primarily good preachers and pastors, and secondarily scholars." Rhee, "Creativity, Integration, and Solidarity," 260–261.

27. The participles state how the nations are to be discipled. Note Lenski, "Two participles of means then state *how* all nations are to be made into disciples: by baptizing them and by teaching them." Lenski, *Interpretation of St. Matthew's Gospel,* 1173.

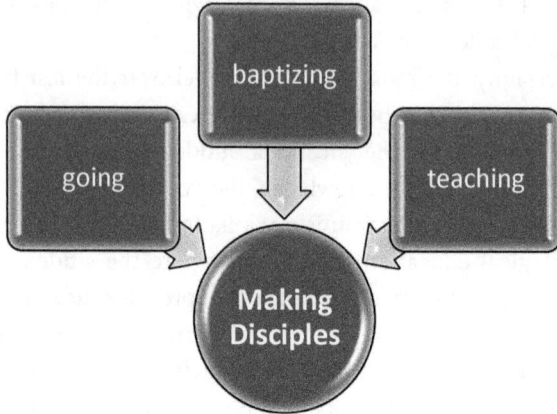

The first participle is "go" [πορευθέντες: *poreuthentes*]. The participle is in the aorist, probably with an inceptive nuance, and carrying an imperatival force.[28] The pre-condition of making disciples is "going." The order is not accidental. We need to be there. This is the indispensable condition of mission, and also, I will suggest, of theological education. Theological education ideally needs to occur within mission or ministry. It is here where Banks' missional model—the Jerusalem model—proves enlightening. Banks is critical of the academic and vocational models, and even argues that we need to go beyond a missiological orientation to in-service instruction. "What is primarily lacking in seminaries," he writes, "is in-ministry formation."[29] Students need to be taken out of the classroom to engage in mission, where they will be instructed as they do ministry.[30] Perhaps it may be appropriate here to quote a

28. Morris, *Gospel according to Matthew*, 746.

29. Banks, *Reenvisioning Theological Education*, 135.

30. However, one also should note the limitations of this model as a wholesale paradigm for theological education. It is difficult to take theological training totally out of the college into the church. First, there remains the aspect of "coming aside" or of "leaving the world" for a while to draw near to God for the purpose of preparation for mission. Also, in practical terms, a church or even a group of churches is not able to provide the expertise and depth of experience that is found in a theological college. And finally, it is still important for students to receive a "credentialed" award for recognition. Banks is aware of

Chinese proverb: "Tell me, and I will forget; show me, and I may remember; involve me, and I will understand."[31]

Another aspect of "going" or "being there" with respect to theological education is the importance of contextualization. The gospel, or theology, should be adapted to speak clearly and pointedly to various cultures and local contexts. Unless there is a process of enculturation, understanding of the gospel will at best be superficial, and at worst, meaningless. With the increasing influence of globalization and centralization, it is becoming more of a challenge to develop theological education that is in tune with the needs of a local culture. Globalization, or dare we say the MacDonaldization of theological education, is working against contextualization.[32] Sometimes, the content of the curriculum, often dominated by Western philosophical concerns, is irrelevant to the local realities.[33] Within Asia, theological education needs to serve a wide range of cultural groups. Theological education needs to become "incarnate" within the focus culture and "be there" in order to be a true servant of the church's mission.[34] Many Asian theologians have emphasized this crucial need for contextualization. Vinay Samuel, Indian missiologist and theologian, commented:

---

these practical issues and does make allowances for them.

31. For better or worse, the Chinese *ethos* has always been a practical one. The most modern expression of this *ethos* is Deng Xiao Ping's famous dictum, "It does not matter if the cat is white or black, so long as it catches mice."

32. "Globalization produces hybridity and commodification." Samuel, "Globalization and Theological Education," 71.

33. Theological education orientated to Western contexts remains a stumbling block for non-Western cultures. See Robinson, "Re-orientation of Theological Education for a Relevant Ministry," 46.

34. Cross-cultural communication or contextualization does not just relate the cognitive aspect (content) of the Christian faith, but also to the behavioral and the appearance of faith (form). Character and behavior have been conditioned by culture. Communication takes place on several levels. Often it is at the behavioral side where there is a communication gap in cross-cultural context. That is why effective ministry should always become indigenous to the specific local and cultural environment.

The more I see and meet with seminary students, the more I get depressed about how irrelevant the content they are learning is to the realities of the world they have to assist.[35]

Similarly, Yau-Man Siew agrees:

. . . a blind copy of Western models with a wholesale incorporation of curriculum and philosophy of training without thoughtful critique and recognition of contextual differences is disastrous.[36]

The second clause of the Great Commission underscores the importance of personal commitment to a new relationship or community. Baptizing into the name [βαπτίζοντες αὐτοὺς εἰς τὸ ὄνομα: *baptizontes autous eis to onoma*] of the Father, Son, and Holy Spirit indicates relationship. The new believer in Jesus enters into a relationship with the triune God and the new community of the kingdom. Baptism incorporates the social aspect of new Christian existence. The Christian life must be experienced and lived out within the community. With respect to theological education, this aspect of the commission will be seen in the building of community, which was one of the emphases of the so-called "Athens model" of theological education. Although building community is becoming increasingly difficult in today's segmented and mobile world, theological colleges need to find ways to foster community. After all, ministry occurs within community. Ignoring this aspect of Christian existence and development will produce dysfunctional pastors and church workers.

The third clause underscores the importance of teaching, and as such is particularly significant for the purposes of the present study. The third participial clause, "teaching them" [διδάσκοντες αὐτούς: *didaskontes autous*], is directly related to the task of education. Teaching is the core business of theological education and implies a body of authoritative knowledge which must be passed on to students. The legitimate concern about authoritative tradition

35. Samuel, "Globalization and Theological Education," 71.

36. Siew, "Curriculum Model," 146.

is reflected in the Geneva or confessional model of theological education. But it is important to reflect carefully about the method and the goals of teaching. The goal of teaching is for students to become disciples, followers of the master, and indeed become like the Lord Jesus himself. The Gospels must play a central role in the curriculum. It is in the Gospels where we meet the crucified and risen Lord. There can be no greater challenge for the task of theological education. This implies that the teacher has already begun to walk the road of a disciple. In particular, teachers need to emulate the Lord in their lives and certainly in their teachings. Martin Goldsmith writes, "As Jesus is the teacher, so the call of the disciples is to follow him in teaching and thus in making disciples/learners."[37] The Gospels present Jesus preeminently as a teacher. Why did he teach? What did he teach? How did he teach?[38] The theological lecturer must be concerned with these questions. Teachers need to learn from modern pedagogy, but theological education needs to remain true to its own presuppositions. What is biblical, or what is Christ-like, about our teaching and the way we teach? Answering these questions would need much more space than is available now. I will simply touch on one or two aspects here.

Making disciples involves relationship; it is more than just the imparting of knowledge. Commenting on the main verb of the passage, Ernst Lohmeyer suggests that the more personal word "discipling" replaced the impersonal word "preaching" as a reflection of how Jesus' went about his task.[39] Mentoring relationships must define the church's task of "making disciples." Theological educators need to develop relationships with their students. To quote McEwan:

> I believe that Trinitarian theology informs us that we are essentially "beings-in-community"; thus, relationship lies at the core of what it means to be human—both relationship with God and with my neighbor. If this is true, then human potential from a Christian perspective can

37. Goldsmith, *Matthew and Mission*, 204.
38. For example, see Holland, "Jesus, a Model for Ministry."
39. Lohmeyer cited in Bruner, *Matthew*, 1097.

never be reached by the isolated "self" being addressed by books and images, whether delivered conventionally or by cyberspace . . .

The role of the teacher is not simply to speak the words or point to the resources that instruct, but also to share the educational journey with the student. We take seriously the role of personal relationship in forming and shaping persons in Christlikeness. This means that we are as concerned for the being of our student as we are for the doing of our student in ministry.[40]

Furthermore, making disciples means to teach transformationally. For transformation to occur, teaching must be in-service, intentional, and creative. "In-service" relates not only to specific ministry contexts but also to daily life. The primary purpose of teaching is to make disciples of the Lord, not to enable students to do research, write scholarly papers, or pass exams. If teachers are to be effective in this task of teaching, they need to leave the classroom (or be creative in bringing the real world into the classroom) Teaching for transformation must be intentional and in context. Transformation does not occur automatically. Naturally, the soil produces weeds. We may conclude by quoting Judith and Sherwood Lingenfelter on transformational teaching:

Biblical transformation involves suffering, repentance, commitment, and practice doing what Jesus has commanded. The classroom is the least effective place for this to occur. Students who have learned to survive by copying copious notes, memorizing them, and regurgitating them on tests cannot understand or appreciate different ways of doing things because they do not see the payoff.[41]

Numerous examples can be cited from the Gospels to illustrate how transformation can occur through the teachings and power of Jesus. The teacher of theology needs to be acquainted with these examples and be able to convey their transforming power to the

---

40. McEwan, "Quality Theological Education," 105, 104.

41. Lingenfelter, *Teaching Cross-Culturally*, 97–98.

classroom and the real world. Theological education will then be more than simply writing papers and passing exams.

A careful study of the Great Commission provides a coherent as well as a comprehensive theology of theological education for the church in Asia. It combines the strengths of the traditional models into an integrated whole and takes the local setting seriously with its emphasis on contextualization. But what is more, it is essentially missiological since it focuses on the urgent need of making disciples. In this way, churches in Asia may develop a particularly Asian theological education that is true to the gospel and that reflects biblical Christianity.

Towards a Theology of Suffering

PRELIMINARY OBSERVATIONS

SINCE DISCIPLESHIP LIES AT the heart of theological education, it is vital that students of theology develop a comprehensive, biblical understanding of what it means to be a disciple as well as the skills and character to make disciples. Discipleship is, of course, a huge topic, and it is not possible to provide an adequate overview of biblical teaching on the subject in this short study.[1] However, since one of the most fundamental aspects of being a disciple—cross-bearing or suffering—is so often neglected today, there is an urgent need to rediscover and highlight the importance of this topic for theological education and ministry.

There are at least two reasons for this need. Firstly, because suffering is an important aspect of biblical teaching as well as life, students of theology need to develop a mature understanding of the place of suffering in the Christian life and ministry. And, secondly, because there is so much misinformation about suffering, especially in some parts of the church in the West, theological students need to be well-equipped to respond to unbalanced views, attitudes, and practices. It is often taught or insinuated that God does not want us to suffer, that suffering is evil, or that suffering is the result of sin or a lack of faith in our lives. Instead, it is suggested that mature and Spirit-filled Christians do not suffer but

1. The New Testament Gospels and the Epistles are basically user manuals on discipleship. See Longenecker, *Patterns of Discipleship in the New Testament*; and Wright, *Following Jesus*.

have victorious and pain-free lives. In short, a prevailing cultural myth is that Christians should not experience suffering in their lives.[2] This mindset is often associated with the so-called "prosperity gospel" or "health-and-wealth gospel." However, when we look at biblical teaching, the picture is quite different from these postmodern Christian myths.

As we will see, understanding and accepting the place of suffering in the Christian life is a central aspect of discipleship. Since this crucial topic is often neglected in some Christian circles, which results in a misunderstanding of Christianity as well as much confusion in the lives of Christians, it is therefore critical that theological students develop a sound theology of suffering—traditionally referred to as *theologia crucis* ("theology of the cross")—in their training and ministry formation. Theological educators need to dispel many misunderstandings and myths regarding the topic of suffering within the Christian life. The view that Christians can live without suffering is not only unbiblical, but it can also have devastating effects on a Christian's spiritual well-being and witness. Ken Wytsma states:

> Without a theology of suffering, we will assume something is wrong, broken, or out of balance whenever we face trials. We may then find ourselves wavering, frantically searching for prosperity and blessing that we believe is the Christian experience, rather than obediently moving forward in the steps of the Savior.[3]

---

2. In his excellent outline of biblical teaching on suffering, Ken Williams lists the following myths about suffering in the Christian life: (1) As Christians, we should not suffer in this life; (2) When we are living in his will, living godly lives, we should experience few hardships; (3) Suffering means something is wrong. It is an abnormal state; (4) Suffering has no redeeming or positive results; (5) Suffering means we can have no joy. It robs us of the choice to rejoice; (6) Spiritual people don't hurt emotionally when they suffer; (7) If God really loves us, he won't let us suffer very much. His love means that he will put a hedge around us to keep terrible trials from entering our lives; (8) When we do suffer, God is punishing us out of anger. He is vindictive and wants us to suffer when he is angry with us. See Williams, "Toward a Biblical Theology of Suffering."

3. Wytsma, "Understanding a Theology of Suffering," lines 1–4.

Therefore, it is important that Christians, especially pastors and teachers, have a mature and biblical understanding of suffering.

Suffering has not been a stranger to the Asian church. Throughout its history, the church in Asia has experienced many struggles and at times horrific persecution. It is often forgotten that hundreds of thousands of Asian Christians were killed by Shapur II (309–79) and Tamerlane (1336–1405) across Mesopotamia and Central Asia. We are more familiar with the severe persecutions in India and Japan, where thousands of Christians were slaughtered because of their faith in the sixteenth and seventeenth centuries. Even today, the church in Asia experiences much opposition, as Jung Sung Rhee observes:

> In our region, the situation is quite different from that of America. We are confronted everyday with non-Christian powers. These are religious and ideological powers, which endanger our Christian identity. We are living in a world of Christian-non-Christian duality, which makes it difficult for us to live only as Jesus' followers. This duality is also found in Western countries, but it is a different kind of duality. We are threatened by the world powers because we are witnessing to Jesus Christ. We are threatened, discriminated against, listed as suspicious citizens, and treated as traitors.[4]

However, this experience of suffering should not be surprising, since the Gospels reveal that it is one of the characteristics of the true followers of Jesus.[5]

The following discussion will make three observations that are foundational for a biblical theology of suffering. It will then provide a short exposition of Matt 16:24, one of the key Gospel texts defining what it means to be a disciple. The discussion will conclude with some practical observations.

---

4. Rhee, "Creativity, Integration, and Solidarity," 261.

5. Also see Yewangoe, *Theologia Crucis in Asia*.

UNDERSTANDING THE HUMAN CONDITION

Firstly, the Bible teaches that God created a perfect world, but due to humanity's rebellion all of creation has been disfigured and has become subject to disorder, struggle, and pain (Gen 3:15–19; also cf. Pss 69:29; 132:1; Ecc 1:3, 8; 2:18–23; 3:1–8; 9:12). Only at the restoration of the New Heaven and Earth will all pain the removed (Rev 21:4). The New Testament also asserts the presence of hardship, illness, and suffering in the life of Christians (Matt 9:36; 11:28; Mark 1:34–39; 8:2; 13:7–8; Luke 13:1–5; Phil 2:26; 1 Thess 2:9; 2 Thess 3:8–10; 2 Tim 3:1–8; 4:20; Jas 5:14–15). In other words, the Bible assumes that life is hard, and that various forms of suffering are part of the human condition and environment. This fact is not only taught in the Bible; it is also, of course, the reality that everyone experiences in life. To be human and to live in this world means to suffer.[6] All the great thinkers and poets of world civilization have expressed this human predicament in various forms. Christians experience suffering because, like all other people, they are human and live in a less-than-perfect world. Therefore, the suffering of Christians should not come as a surprise or be regarded as something abnormal. It is only with the second coming of Christ in the New Heaven and Earth that suffering will no longer be part of the human condition.

UNDERSTANDING THE GOSPEL

Secondly, the basis of a Christian theology of suffering lies in the life and ministry of Jesus. Who is Jesus? What did he come to do? What is the gospel? What is the essence of Christianity? Of course, there are no questions of greater importance than these for Christians and students of theology. When we turn to the Gospels in the

---

6. A related issue is the problem of evil or theodicy, which simply stated asks, "Why do bad things happen to good people?" We will not deal with it here. See Boyd, *Is God to Blame?*; Davis, *Encountering Evil*; Hall, *God and Human Suffering*; Hasker, *Triumph of God Over Evil*; Piper and Taylor, *Suffering and the Sovereignty of God*.

New Testament, we discover that they were written precisely to answer these fundamental questions.

Most scholars believe that Mark was the first Gospel to be written. Even though it seems that Mark, or the author of the second Gospel that appears in modern Bibles, was not an accomplished Greek writer, he had an overwhelming burden to write his book about Jesus. Why did Mark write his Gospel, since many stories about Jesus were circulating all over the Roman Empire?[7] With a careful study of the Gospel of Mark, the answer is transparent. Mark wanted to show, more than anything else, that Jesus was not just a miracle worker or a great teacher, but that he came to suffer and die on the cross. The culmination of the Gospel's story is found in the last few days of Jesus' life, which climaxed in the cross and resurrection. Even though Jesus probably lived for more than thirty years, Mark's story about Jesus describes only a short period of his life, and hones in on the last few days of his passion. The Gospel of Mark is not a biography of Jesus; rather, it is a Gospel, which proclaims the good news that Jesus came "to give his life as a ransom for many" (Mark 10:45). In fact, 40 percent of Mark's content relates the last two days of Jesus' life—how he suffered under the hands of the Roman soldiers and the Jewish authorities, and how he was crucified on Golgotha just outside the wall of Jerusalem. There is no doubt where Mark's emphasis lies. Three times in the Gospel, Jesus predicts that he will suffer and die, and then be raised on the third day (Mark 8:31; 9:31; 10:32–34). Jesus' unique title, the Son of Man, is closely related to his suffering and hence his authority to forgive sins (Mark 2:10–11). In fact, everything in the Gospel story relates or refers to the cross and the resurrection. And, according to Mark, this was to fulfill the Old Testament prophecies (cf. Mark 1:2–3; 11:9–10; 12:10–11; 14:26–27; 15:34). The cross stands as the foundation, center, and goal of Jesus' ministry. Without the cross, people cannot understand Jesus correctly; without the cross, there is no gospel; without the cross, there is no atonement for sin and salvation. Therefore,

7. For a more detailed discussion see, Ferreira, "Markan Outline and Emphases."

the cross and a theology of suffering stand at the core of the Christian message. Suffering is not just part of the human condition and environment; it lies at the heart of the gospel message. This is the main point of the Gospels' Christology which every disciple must understand and embrace (cf. Matt 13:23; Mark 4:20; Luke 8:15).

This emphasis that we see in the Gospel of Mark is similarly strong in the other Gospels, as well as in the rest of the New Testament. The key point here is that suffering and the related doctrine of substitutionary atonement stands at the heart of New Testament teaching.[8] Therefore, there can be no such thing as a "Christless Christianity"; it is a contradiction in terms.[9] The problem with the popular message of the prosperity "gospel" preachers is that they do not focus on the Christ who was crucified.

UNDERSTANDING DISCIPLESHIP

Thirdly, Jesus' central teaching on discipleship, the major focus of theological education, is largely an expression of a theology of suffering. Perhaps the second most important question that the Gospel writers answer, which is closely related to the first, is: What is a Christian? What does it mean to be a follower and a disciple of Jesus? Again, only a biblical theology of discipleship should be legitimate for the church and Christians today. When we turn to the Gospels, we note that a major component of Jesus' teachings revolved around the topic of discipleship. The most important teaching of Jesus about discipleship, or his definition of discipleship, which comes directly after he talked about his own suffering

---

8. This traditional teaching of orthodox Christianity has been challenged recently. For example, Steve Chalke attacked the idea of penal substitution by saying that, "The cross isn't a form of cosmic child abuse—a vengeful Father punishing his Son for an offense he has not even committed." See Chalke, *Lost Message of Jesus*, 182. Also see, Wallace and Rusk, *Moral Transformation*, and Finlan, *Problems with Atonement*. For a response to these criticisms, see Wolterstorff, *Justice in Love*; Moser, *Elusive God*; Jeffery, Ovey, and Sach, *Pierced for our Transgressions*; and Tidball, Hilborn, and Thacker, *Atonement Debate*.

9. See Horton, *Christless Christianity*.

and death, involves suffering (Mark 8:34; Luke 14:25–33; Matt 10:38; 16:24; 27:32, 40, 42). Just as suffering was a central aspect of Jesus' ministry, so too it is an essential requirement for discipleship. In other words, there can be no discipleship without suffering. Indeed, Jesus spent much time preparing his followers for the challenges they would face in the future.

The presence of suffering in the life of the Christian is also a major theme in Acts and the Epistles of the New Testament (e.g., Acts 14:22; Phil 1:29; 2 Tim 3:12; Heb 12:3–11; Jas 1:2–4; 1 Pet 1:5–7; 3:8–17; Rev 6–8). When we observe how Paul understood and experienced his own ministry, suffering becomes even more prominent (1 Cor 2:3–5; 4:9–13; 2 Cor 4:7–12; 11:21–33; Col 1:24). Of course, much more can be said about the reasons and purposes of suffering in the Christian life, but we just want to make the point here that all the New Testament authors emphasize that suffering is a central aspect of the Christian life.

THE GOSPEL'S KEY TEACHING ABOUT DISCIPLESHIP

Since the statement about taking up the cross is central in Jesus' understanding of discipleship, and occurs several times in the Gospels, it is important to study it carefully. The Gospel of Matthew, like the other Gospels, contains much material on discipleship; but perhaps the most important statement that may serve to underscore the fundamental elements of Christian discipleship occurs in Matt 16:24, just after the most important Christological affirmation of the Gospel (cf. Matt 10:38; Mark 8:34; Luke 9:23). The lessons here are universal and always applicable to Christian life and ministry:

> Then Jesus told his disciples, "If anyone would come after me, let him deny himself and take up his cross and follow me."

In this passage, Jesus outlines three principles, or three steps, for those who wish to become his disciples. The first principle is about denying something. The second principle is about carrying something. And the third principle is about following someone. The following sequence appears.

deny ▶ carry ▶ follow

These principles are all related to the disciple's worldview, spiritual attitude, and inner character. We are all very much aware that much knowledge and many skills are needed for ministry. We often talk about the head, the hand, and the heart in terms of ministry formation. But of these three, the most critical aspect for the Christian life and for ministry, as mentioned previously, is the heart. The steps that Jesus outlines here about discipleship involve matters of the heart; he is teaching about the basics of the Christian life and ministry. Theological educators do need to concern themselves with the head and the hand, but much more importantly, they need to focus on the heart.

The first principle for ministry is about "denying" something. The aorist imperative *aparneomai* [ἀπαρνέομαι] denotes a decisive decision to utterly reject or deny something. What must be denied? Yourself! This is the first principle of the Christian life. It is also the first step of becoming a true minister or missionary of the Lord. Theological students and pastors must deny fleshly lusts. When their "flesh" wants to hate, envy, or gossip, they must reject the inclination. Indeed, they must deny themselves the room to harbor these attitudes and behaviors and say "No!" to these things. When Potiphar's wife made lewd advances to Joseph, he ran away and escaped. They must also learn to deny worldly desires. The "world" tempts us to be rich, to be powerful, to be famous, to become callous and live lives of comfort and ease. Pastors must say "No!" to these things.[10] Abraham was prepared to leave the security of family and the comfortable life of the city to travel all the way to Canaan

10. In the code of Professional Ethics for Ministers in Appendix 2, the principles of beneficence and integrity often require the abandonment of personal preferences and desires.

and to take up the lifestyle of a wanderer. Moses rejected the attractions of Egyptian high society to associate with the suffering of God's people. Sometimes pastors even need to deny that which is right and proper in order to engage in gospel ministry and fulfil their calling. For example, in obeying the Lord's call, they often decline more lucrative positions or remain in poorer regions despite opportunities to move to better surroundings. In short, those who aspire to be disciples of Jesus, and much more those who desire to be ministers and missionaries of the Lord, must make a decision to die. The dead are not tempted to commit adultery and fornication. The dead are not jealous of the living. The dead do not gossip or have fits of rage and anger. Indeed, a cemetery is a very peaceful place; there is no adultery, fornication, jealousy, fights, or gossip there!

The second principle for ministry is about "carrying" something. If we have learned the lesson of denying ourselves, we can proceed to the second step. Whereas the first principle is negative, it relates to what disciples must reject, the second principle is positive, it relates to what disciples must take up and embrace. Since disciples have rejected fleshly lusts and worldly ambitions, their hands are empty to take up and embrace something else. And what must be taken up? The cross! The Greek aorist imperative *airō* [αἴρω] also indicates a decisive decision to embrace the suffering of the cross. Christianity is extraordinary. Ministry is radical. It is not for the half-hearted. As people say, "If you can't take the heat in the kitchen, then get out." As mentioned earlier, it is significant that Jesus' teaching about ministry comes immediately after the first passion prediction in the Gospel of Matthew. As there can be no Christianity without the cross, there can be no discipleship without suffering. For Jesus, the cross was the indispensable element of his ministry. So too, there cannot be genuine discipleship, let alone real Christian ministry, without a cross.

What does the "cross" mean? Practically speaking, it means many things. The first thing it means is "shame." In the ancient world, execution by crucifixion was the pinnacle of dishonor and humiliation. Disciples must be prepared for scorn and ridicule.

Secondly, it means repentance and faith. In ministry, Christians need to embrace these things as opportunities that qualify them for discipleship. Thirdly, it means to accept others who are different from you. A disciple must suspend judgment. Fourthly, it means to love God and serve others. They must be content to take the lower position, stand aside, and defer to the wishes of others. Fifthly, it means to endure persecution for the sake of Jesus and kingdom values. Theological students must learn to say "Yes!" to such things. It is also interesting to note that the Gospel of Luke adds the word "daily." Since there are going to be new challenges every day in the Christian life and ministry, students must be taught to make daily decisions of commitment to cross-bearing. When the nineteenth-century existentialist, Søren Kierkegaard, noticed how the clergy were preoccupied with their stipend, he exclaimed, " . . . there is literally not one single honest priest!"[11] It is only authentic Christian lives which have any witness and influence in the world.

We may also notice the possessive pronoun in "his cross," suggesting that there is a different cross for each one to bear. The burdens and challenges that Christians need to embrace for the sake of gospel ministry are all different, but the principle is the same. John the Baptist embraced the desert. Paul embraced long travels, beatings, and imprisonments. The Apostle John embraced the loneliness and isolation of Patmos. In modern times, we also have many bright examples of Christians who said "Yes!" to the cross. The Chinese evangelist Wang Mingdao preferred to be jailed rather than to deny his Lord. The Japanese evangelist Toyohiko Kagawa accepted ridicule and lived among the poor to show the love of Christ. The Indian evangelist Bakht Singh Chabra accepted rejection by his family and lived on the streets for the sake of his Christian profession.

The third principle for ministry is about "following" someone. On the one hand, students of theology must learn to say "No!" and, on the other hand, they must also learn to say "Yes!"—but then finally, when they have mastered these principles, they can

11. Kierkegaard, *Attack upon "Christendom,"* 229.

go on to the most exciting step of discipleship and ministry; namely, following Jesus. The Greek present imperative *akoloutheō* [ἀκολουθέω] indicates that the ongoing "following" of Jesus is the ultimate aim of discipleship; self-denial or suffering is not an end in itself, but the prerequisite for something more important. Christians do not glorify suffering, or actively seek suffering for the sake of suffering. Rather, their main aim is to follow Jesus, but following Jesus will sometimes, inevitably, require suffering.

The next thing that we need to note in this final expression is that discipleship is not about a cause, a set of teachings, or a theological tradition; rather, it is about Jesus. In other words, students should be taught to become zealous about Jesus, and not so much about Calvin, Wesley, Moody, or Watchman Nee. They need to know Jesus and learn how to imitate him in their daily lives. This is indeed the most amazing life and ministry that one can have. Therefore, the key principle of discipleship and ministry is about following Jesus. (It is not just about saying "No!" or saying "Yes!"; it is about saying "Wow!") When they follow Jesus, people are changed and the world is transformed. When Francis of Assisi turned his back on the world to follow Jesus in simplicity and purity, thousands were affected. When Mother Theresa left the comfort of Europe to serve the poor in Calcutta, she brought healing, hope, and inspiration to millions. The Gospels and church history are replete with stories like this. Discipleship is about walking and living with Jesus. It is about experiencing his power, peace, and joy. Ministry is about healing the sick, casting out demons, and reversing the work of the devil. It is about introducing people to Jesus and bringing the power of God's kingdom into the lives of people. It is about seeing miracles and feeding thousands with two fish and five loaves. It is about walking on the water. It is about turning the world upside down.

PRACTICAL CONSIDERATIONS

Since suffering is an important part of the life of discipleship according to biblical teaching (as well as our own experience), it is important for students of theology to develop a sound biblical theology of suffering. Otherwise, they may misrepresent Christianity (whether the gospel or discipleship) as prosperity preachers often do, and cause much hurt when people face weakness, failure, and hardship in their lives.[12] With an inadequate theology of suffering, pastors may also become disillusioned when they are faced with suffering (either the suffering of others or their own). The main aim of this short discussion is to underscore the reality and presence of suffering within the Christian life. It is not abnormal or necessarily the result of sin or unbelief. In fact, suffering is often the will of God for our lives. We should reject the postmodern and Western Christian myth that suffering has no place in the Christian life. It is therefore necessary for teachers of theology in all areas of the theological curriculum (biblical studies, theology, history, counselling, pastoral care, missiology, etc.) to equip students with a sound theology of suffering and to prepare them to face the inevitable challenges of Christian life and ministry. Every lecturer needs to imbibe and project the college's vision and *ethos*.

In fact, when we reflect more deeply on the Great Commission, we realize that each step required for the fulfillment of the main command to make disciples, expressed by the three subordinate participles, involves suffering. "Going" implies leaving one's place of security and comfort, crossing boundaries, long journeys, and taking risks. The sacrament of baptism implies "dying with Christ" and sacrificial commitment to a network of new relationships. Teaching and learning are also hard and require discipline and perseverance. Those who commit themselves to theological education must be prepared to expend the cost if they want to be successful.

Having established the important place of suffering in the Christian life and ministry, one may go on to reflect more deeply and prayerfully on several related questions. For example, why is suffering a part of the Christian life? Why do Christians suffer? What kind of suffering do Christians experience? What is the purpose of suffering? How should we respond to suffering? And how can we help, support, and encourage others who are experiencing suffering? I do not have the space to address these

---

12. See the statement on Spiritual Abuse in Appendix 3.

questions here, but I may provide a short summary of the kinds of suffering people experience in life.

From a theological point of view, we may observe that in general the Bible distinguishes between two kinds of suffering: (1) common human suffering and (2) specifically Christian suffering. Common human suffering is experienced by everyone, Christians and non-Christians alike, and, as we have pointed out, is part of the human condition. It incorporates suffering such as loss, fear, sadness, anxiety, illness, weakness, failure, bereavement, toil, hardship, etc. People often suffer as the direct result of their own sin, but suffering is also often brought about by economic crises, disasters, wars, exploitation, and discrimination. Specifically Christian suffering is suffering that results from being a Christian; that is, suffering for the sake of the gospel. In general, there are three categories of Christian suffering. Firstly, sanctification involves aspects of suffering, such as discipline: the rejection of fleshly and worldly desires, fasting, and prayer. Secondly, Christian ministry and service often involve measures of suffering, such as helping the needy, financial sacrifice, time, toil, busyness, ministry responsibilities and pressures, concern for the wellbeing of others, and personal weaknesses and regrets in ministry. Thirdly, Christians are sometimes persecuted because of their commitment to Jesus and the gospel. Persecution may be verbal, emotional, physical, social, or economic (e.g., rejection, shame, denouncement, ridicule, physical abuse, imprisonment, and even death). In other words, it is impossible to be alive and not suffer. It is also impossible to be a Christian and not experience Christian suffering; there cannot be true discipleship without cross-bearing.

Common Human Suffering	Special Christian Suffering

In sanctification

Hardships, illnesses, disasters, exploitation, wars, etc.

In ministry

In persecution

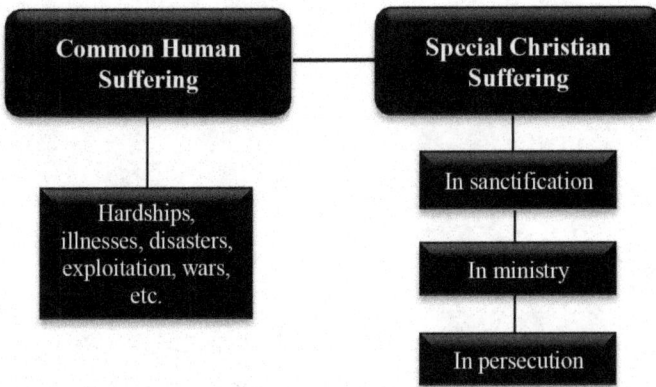

Therefore, we conclude that the topic of suffering, or a theology of suffering, should also feature prominently in the curriculum of theological education. Of course, this can be done in a variety of ways. A distinct unit can be devoted to the subject, and it may also be integrated in the teaching of other units in the areas of biblical studies, theology, church history, or counselling. The topic of suffering may also feature in the spiritual formation program of theological colleges, such as in prayer, chapel, devotion, and special seminars.[13]

13. A suggested seminar on the topic of suffering may contain the following parts: (1) Biblical Foundations (where students study the teaching on the subject in the Gospels) and (2) Practical Implications (where students reflect on their own experiences or observations of suffering).

Conclusion

THEOLOGICAL EDUCATION IS ONE of the most exciting and important tasks in which to be engaged; it lies at the very heart of the Great Commission. Theological education fulfils the Great Commission both directly as it "makes disciples" and indirectly as it equips the church to "make disciples." Considering the contingencies surrounding theological education today, the Great Commission may empower and enlighten us. The justification of theological education lies in the authority of Jesus, the crucified and risen Lord. The content of theological education centers on him, the one who challenges us to follow wherever he will lead and to be transformed into his image. The method of theological education involves participation in his mission, sharing in his fellowship, and keeping his commandments. In other words, theological education must be Christocentric; it must be both intensely personal and communal; it must be transformational; and it must be missional. The only adequate theology for theological education is a biblical one. Without this direct connection with the commission of the risen Lord, theological education is robbed of its power and significance. Theological education will always do well when it holds to its historical roots.

We have also seen that since a biblical theology of theological education based on the Great Commission focuses on discipleship, the development of a theology of suffering is an important aspect of theological education. Theological students need to become disciples of Jesus, and then become disciple makers, which means that they must not only understand but also embrace the word of the cross (Mark 4:20; cf. Matt 13:23). It is only then that they will become mature disciples and bear much fruit in the Christian life and ministry. The willingness to suffer for the sake of the gospel is one of the key signs of being a true disciple of Jesus and has also been a characteristic mark of the church in Asia. Asian Christians need to resist the influence of western postmodernism and hold to this element of biblical and historical Christianity. Only the real biblical gospel message can meet the deepest human needs and address the challenges of Asian society, inspiring true faith and hope for the future. Jesus concludes the Great Commission with the promise of his presence: "And behold, I am with you every day, until the end of the age" (Matt 28:20). With the presence and empowerment of the Lord, the mission of the church in Asia will be fulfilled.

Appendix 1

Graduate Attributes[1]

GRADUATE ATTRIBUTES ARE THE characteristics, attitudes, and skills that students should possess upon completion of their training program at theological colleges. The training programs at colleges are geared towards achieving these outcomes. They reflect the vision, values, and *ethos* of the college. They also communicate to the wider Christian community what it may expect from college graduates in ministry and mission.

Graduates are expected to demonstrate the following attributes:

1. THEY WILL BE PASSIONATE DISCIPLES OF JESUS CHRIST

Graduates will maintain a vibrant relationship with God, be passionate about following Jesus, and walk by the Spirit in every area of life. They will seek to love God above all else and others as themselves in their attitudes, words, and deeds. They will imitate Jesus, obey his Word, deny themselves, take up their crosses, and follow Jesus wherever he may lead (Mark 8:34).

---

1. This set of Graduate Attributes is based on those adopted by Crossway College (now Brisbane School of Theology) in 2009.

2. THEY WILL HAVE A SOUND KNOWLEDGE OF THE BIBLE

Graduates will have an in-depth and comprehensive knowledge of the Bible. They will be committed to the infallibility and authority of the Bible as God's Word in everything pertaining to salvation and the Christian life (2 Tim 3:14–17). They will do their best to be good teachers of the Bible who correctly explain the word of truth (2 Tim 2:15).

3. THEY WILL HAVE GENUINE HUMILITY AND DEMONSTRATE FAITHFULNESS IN LIFE AND MINISTRY

Graduates will live lives of holiness, prayer, humility, and faithfulness. They will be willing to acknowledge their shortcomings and mistakes and be open to receive constructive criticism and advice. They will do nothing out of selfish ambition, but in humility will consider others better than themselves (Phil 2:3). They will be prepared to suffer for the sake of Christ, knowing that "we must go through many hardships to enter the kingdom of God" (Acts 14:22).

4. THEY WILL BE EFFECTIVE COMMUNICATORS OF THE GOSPEL

Graduates will know the gospel and will be eager and able to communicate the gospel, especially in word, but also through writing and other media, in ways that are culturally sensitive and intelligible to others. They will have compassionate hearts, listening empathetically to people in their particular contexts. They will be ready to preach the Word at any time with patience and care (2 Tim 4:2), trying to persuade people to believe the gospel and to become followers of Jesus (2 Cor 5:11).

5. THEY WILL HAVE A GREAT COMMITMENT TO GOD'S MISSION

Graduates will be aware of the needs and opportunities of local and global mission. They will endeavor to see the coming of God's kingdom in every sphere of life, strive for justice for the poor, and work towards community transformation. They will be passionately committed to and active in working towards the fulfilment of the Great Commission, which is to make disciples of all nations (Matt 28:18–20).

6. THEY WILL BE COMMITTED TO TEAM MINISTRY AND SERVANT LEADERSHIP

Graduates will be committed to the local church as the family of God and as their context for ministry and base for mission (Heb 10:24–25). They will work enthusiastically and cooperatively with others in ministry teams. They will be open to Christians across various evangelical denominations and churches (Luke 9:49–50). As leaders they will be disciple-makers, following the Lord Jesus in serving, leading by example, and training and mentoring other leaders (Mark 10:43–45).

7. THEY WILL BE COMPETENT IN BASIC MINISTRY SKILLS

Graduates will be competent in basic ministry skills, including preaching, teaching, leading, and caring for people. They will use their gifts to implement constructive change in the church and community (1 Tim 4:6–16). They will be culturally attuned and flexible in dealing with a range of issues (1 Cor 9:19–23). They will embrace accountability and maintain professional standards in various contexts. They will be "salt and light" in the world (Matt 5:13–14) and be able to "prepare God's people for works of service, so that the body of Christ may be built up" (Eph 4:12).

8. THEY WILL BE COMMITTED TO LIFELONG LEARNING AND PERSONAL GROWTH

Graduates will be proactive in expanding their knowledge and abilities. They will be open to new challenges, be willing to face unfamiliar problems, and accept wider responsibilities. They will continue to grow in faith, knowledge, and maturity, "forgetting what is behind and pressing . . . towards the goal for the prize of the upward call of God in Christ Jesus" (Phil 3:13–14).

Appendix 2

Code of Professional Ethics for Ministers[1]

PREAMBLE

THIS CODE IS BASED on the assumption that ministers of the gospel should adhere to the highest ethical and professional standards according to the nature of Christian ministry as defined by the New Testament. The Code articulates the standards to which ministers of the Gospel should subject themselves and aims to protect the church and the general public from the abuse of the ministerial office. As such, on one hand, the Code seeks to curtail incompetence, immaturity, and misconduct in ministry; on the other hand, it seeks to encourage high standards and sound biblical principles in the performance of gospel ministry. As Paul says, "Now it is required of stewards that they be found faithful" (1 Cor 4:2), and "no one is crowned without competing according to the rules" (2 Tim 2:5). Ministers should endeavor in all their conduct and service to glorify the Lord Jesus and to bring honor to the vocation of the gospel minister.

---

1. This code was developed by Eric Liddell Institute in Brisbane in 2014.

FIVE VALUES

The Code is based on five primary values: beneficence, integrity, respect, competence, and responsibility.

1. Beneficence

Ministers' primary motivation in Christian service is to glorify the Lord Jesus Christ and to benefit the church and society. They do not enter Christian ministry for self-advancement or personal gain.

2. Integrity

Ministers maintain truthfulness, honesty, and openness with respect to the motives, standards, and conduct of their ministry. They do not engage in deception, manipulation, or hypocrisy. They recognize when their conduct departs from biblical and professional standards.

3. Respect

Ministers respect and protect the dignity, privacy, confidentiality, and rights of all people they serve or meet. They do not slander or degrade others, or discriminate on the basis of race, culture, gender, disability, socioeconomic status, religion, or theological stance.

4. Competence

Ministers understand the nature and purpose of Christian ministry and are able to carry out their responsibilities effectively. At the same time, they work within the limits of their calling, knowledge, and skills. They value the need for preparation, education, and ongoing training throughout their lives.

5. Responsibility

Ministers recognize that they are responsible to the Lord Jesus, their leadership team, the church, and the larger society in which they serve. They uphold biblical and professional standards and work under the protocols of church and society. Ministers take advice, cooperate, and consult with others.

TEN PRINCIPLES

Beneficence

1. Ministers should strive, first of all, to please the Lord Jesus in all things, even despite personal cost and suffering. The sole purpose of their work is to promote the gospel, the spiritual growth and welfare of the church, the betterment of society, and the cause of the needy. They do not act for the sake of their own reputation, financial gain, or social standing.

2. Ministers should strive to support the work of the gospel and the poor beyond their local ministry context, as is practical. They do not compete with others but are concerned about the wider Christian community and society, not only their own ministry.

Integrity

3. Ministers should strive to maintain theological orthodoxy for the duration of their lives and ministry. They focus their preaching and teaching ministry on the gospel of the Lord Jesus Christ, avoiding peripheral and unprofitable doctrines that often distract and divide the church.

4. Ministers should strive to maintain moral integrity, holiness, and respectable behavior in both their public and private lives. They avoid greed, dishonesty, promiscuity, and unjust behavior. They live pure, upright, and blameless lives, maintaining strict ethical boundaries.

Respect

5. Ministers should strive to honor all people, keep confidentiality, and protect the reputation of others. They do not cause offense, degrade others, and especially do not slander or disparage other gospel ministers and Christian churches. They do not misuse their position to lord it over others but give people freedom as independent human beings who are responsible for their own actions.

Competence

6. Ministers should strive to maintain competence in the performance of their primary duties of preaching the gospel, teaching the Word of God, praying for the needy and the sick, and pastoring and equipping the people of God through the enabling of the Holy Spirit. As such, they will spend much time in prayer, ministry preparation, and ongoing theological training.

7. Ministers should strive to understand their calling to the ministry of the Word and prayer, and as such, they stay within the parameters of their vocation, avoiding matters that lie outside the purview of their role. Therefore, they have clear boundaries regarding their ministry function, and do not engage in matters such as politics, healthcare, financial advice, psychological counselling, social work, etc. Instead, they may refer people to qualified experts, as appropriate.

8. Ministers should strive to grow in the knowledge and grace of the Lord Jesus and develop sound character in accordance with their vocation. They do not harbor bitterness and are not quarrelsome, but instead are forgiving, gentle, and temperate.

Accountability

9. Ministers should strive to work under the accountability structures of the church and the larger Christian community. They understand their role as servant leaders who are part of their ministry team. As such, they do not operate independently but are open to, seek out, and welcome the input of others regarding their ministry performance.

10. Ministers should strive to be humble and considerate in all situations. They are always open to correction; they take advice; and they are proactive in conflict prevention and conflict resolution.

Appendix 3

Spiritual Abuse[1]

PREAMBLE

PERHAPS, PEOPLE ARE NOT familiar with the term "spiritual abuse," but just as there is physical or emotional abuse, spiritual abuse is also very real. Unfortunately, spiritual abuse happens all too frequently in the church and among Christians today, and it can have devastating results for victims, such as distrust, anxiety, low self-esteem, depression, ill health, disillusionment, broken relationships, and deep emotional pain. Spiritual abuse hurts people, discredits the church, and brings dishonor to the ministry of the gospel. The Bible often talks about spiritual abuse among God's people (e.g., Ezek 34:1–10; Zech 11:15–17; Matt 20:25; 23:1–33; Luke 22:24–27; and 1 Pet 5:3) and wants people to experience freedom and joy (e.g., Matt 9:36–38; 11:28–30; Gal 3:1–5; 5:1).

Theological students and church leaders need to be aware of the problem and recognize the characteristics or symptoms of spiritual abuse. It is also critical that our graduates (who will be future pastors and church leaders) are not perpetrators of spiritual abuse but have a mature self-image and sound biblical understanding of

1. This appendix is based on a statement produced by Eric Liddell Institute in 2015.

ministry. Those who perpetrate spiritual abuse often suffer from an inadequate self-image, insecurity, and low self-worth. They also have an unbiblical understanding of the gospel, leadership, and church ministry.

Definition: Spiritual abuse occurs when people in positions of power misuse their authority for selfish interests, personal goals, or for the advancement of their organization at the expense of the freedom, spiritual growth, and emotional well-being of others. The person in the position of power uses "spiritual" means and church power structures to control, manipulate, and restrict the freedom of others. Perpetrators of spiritual abuse tend to be authoritarian and legalistic, and any criticism is deemed to be a sign of disobedience to God.

CHARACTERISTICS OF SPIRITUAL ABUSE

1. **Authoritarian Leadership.** The leader or church does not tolerate any dissent from members, and there is no freedom to question the decisions or the teachings of the leader.

2. **Exclusive Allegiance.** The leader or church demands exclusive commitment from the members. People are not allowed to visit other churches or read unsanctioned material.

3. **Total Control.** All aspects of the church's ministry or members' lives are controlled by the leader. Often, there is an inordinate demand on the time and finances of members.

4. **Exaltation of Leader(s).** The leader is regarded as having special status before God with unique insights into God's will, or having special spiritual powers.

5. **Suppress Criticism.** Criticism is viewed as an attack on the authority of the leader or church and is not tolerated. Any criticism is viewed as disobedience to God.

6. **Culture of Fear and Shame.** Members do not feel free to express what they really think or feel. Those who are "weak" or

do not behave according to the wishes of the leadership are publically shamed.

7. **Unbalanced Teachings and Practices.** Churches or leaders that abuse are often unbalanced in doctrine and practice. They major in minors or have some theological views or practices (which are peripheral to the Christian faith) that are disproportionately emphasized and cannot be questioned.

8. **Lack of Transparency.** There is an atmosphere of secrecy and lack of accountability in the leadership from fear of being questioned or rejected.

CONCLUSION

If a number of these characteristics are present in a church or the leadership style of a pastor, it is likely that members are being spiritually abused. Prayerfully consider, with others, what you may do to address the situation with wisdom, grace, and truth.

Selected Bibliography

Aleshire, Daniel. "The Character and Assessment of Learning for Religious Vocation: MDiv Education and Numbering the Levites." *Theological Education* 30 (2003) 1–15.

Banks, Robert. *Reenvisioning Theological Education: Exploring a Missional Alternative to Current Models.* Grand Rapids: Eerdmans, 1999.

Boyd, Gregory A. *Is God to Blame? Moving Beyond Pat Answers to the Problem of Suffering.* Downers Grove, IL: InterVarsity, 2003.

Bruner, Frederick Dale. *Matthew: A Commentary, Vol. 2: The Churchbook.* Dallas: Word, 1990.

Chalke, Steve, and Alan Mann. *The Lost Message of Jesus.* Grand Rapids: Zondervan, 2003.

Davis, Stephen T. *Encountering Evil: Live Options in Theodicy.* New ed. Louisville, KY: Westminster John Knox, 2001.

Duraisingh, Christopher. "Ministerial Formation for Mission: Implications for Theological Education." *International Review of Mission* 81 (1992) 33–45.

Edgar, Brian. "The Theology of Theological Education." *Evangelical Review of Theology* 29 (2005) 208–17.

Ferreira, Johan. "The Great Commission: Towards a Theology of Theological Education." In *Cultivating Wisdom with the Heart—BCV Chinese Department's 10th Anniversary Anthology of Essays,* edited by Justin Tan, 15–32. Melbourne, AU: Bible College of Victoria, 2006.

———. "The Markan Outline and Emphases." In *Content and Setting of the Gospel Tradition,* edited by Mark Harding and Alanna Nobbs, 263–88. Grand Rapids: Eerdmans, 2010.

Finlan, Stephen. *Problems with Atonement: The Origins of, and Controversy about, the Atonement Doctrine.* Collegeville, MN: Liturgical, 2005.

Foord, Martin. "The Elements of a Theology of Theological Education." In *Theological Education: Foundations, Practices, and Future Directions,* edited by Andrew M. Bain and Ian Hussey, 29–43. Eugene, OR: Wipf & Stock, 2018.

Goldsmith, Martin. *Matthew and Mission: The Gospel through Jewish Eyes.* Carlisle, UK: Paternoster, 2001.

Hall, Douglas John. *God and Human Suffering: An Exercise in the Theology of the Cross*. Minneapolis: Augsburg Fortress, 1986.

Hasker, William. *The Triumph of God Over Evil: Theodicy for a World of Suffering*. Downers Grove, IL: InterVarsity, 2008.

Holland, J.T. "Jesus, a Model for Ministry." *The Journal of Pastoral Care* 36 (1982) 255–64.

Horton, Michael. *Christless Christianity: The Alternative Gospel of American Culture*. Grand Rapids: Baker, 2012.

"ICAA Manifesto on the Renewal of Evangelical Theological Education." *Theological Education Today* 8 (1984) 136–43.

Jeffery, Steve, Mike Ovey, and Andrew Sach. *Pierced for our Transgressions: Rediscovering the Glory of Penal Substitution*. Nottingham, UK: InterVarsity, 2007.

Kelsey, David H. *Between Athens and Berlin: The Theological Education Debate*. Grand Rapids: Eerdmans, 1993.

———. *To Understand God Truly: What's Theological about a Theological School?* Louisville, KY: Westminster John Knox, 1992.

Kierkegaard, Søren. *Kierkegaard's Attack upon "Christendom," 1854–1855*. Translated by Walter Lowrie. Princeton: Princeton University Press, 1946.

Kossen, Peter. "Interpreting and Applying Scripture." *Vox Reformata* 50 (1988) 3–38.

Legge, James. *The Chinese Classics: A Translation, Critical and Exegetical Notes, Prolegomena, and Copious Indexes*. London: Trübner & Co., 1861.

Lenski, R.C.H. *The Interpretation of St. Matthew's Gospel*. Minneapolis: Augsburg Fortress, 1943.

Lingenfelter, Judith, and Sherwood Lingenfelter. *Teaching Cross-Culturally: An Incarnational Model for Learning and Teaching*. Grand Rapids: Baker, 2003.

Longenecker, Richard N., ed. *Patterns of Discipleship in the New Testament*. Grand Rapids: Eerdmans, 1996.

McEwan, David. "Quality Theological Education from a Wesleyan Perspective." *The Mediator* 2, no. 2 (April 2001) 94–108.

Melugin, Roy F. "Texts to Transform Life: Reading Isaiah as Christians." *Word & World* 19, no. 2 (Spring 1999) 109-16.

Morris, Leon. *The Gospel according to Matthew*. Grand Rapids: Eerdmans, 1992.

Moser, Paul K. *The Elusive God: Reorientating Religious Epistemology*. New York: Cambridge University Press, 2009.

Noelliste, Dieumeme. "Handmaiden to God's Economy: Biblical Foundations of Theological Education." In *Leadership in Theological Education, Vol. 1*, edited by Fritz Deininger and Orbelina Eguizabal, 7–31. Carlisle, UK: Langham Global Library, 2017.

Peterson, Michael L. *Philosophy of Education: Issues and Options*. Downers Grove, IL: InterVarsity, 1986.

Piper, John, and Justin Taylor. *Suffering and the Sovereignty of God*. Wheaton, IL: Crossway, 2006.

Rhee, Jung Sung. "Creativity, Integration, and Solidarity in Ministerial Formation in N.E. Asia." *East Asia Journal of Theology* 2 (1984) 259–71.

Selected Bibliography

Robinson, Gnana. "Re-orientation of Theological Education for a Relevant Ministry." *East Asia Journal of Theology* 4 (1986) 46–51.

Samuel, Vinay. "Globalization and Theological Education." *Transformation* 18 (2001) 69–74.

Siew, Yau-Man. "A Curriculum Model for the Evaluation of Existing Programmes of Theological Education in Asia." *Asia Journal of Theology* 9 (1995) 146–69.

Tidball, Derek, David Hilborn, and Justin Thacker, eds. *The Atonement Debate: Papers from the London Symposium on the Theology of Atonement.* Grand Rapids: Zondervan, 2008.

Wallace, A.J., and R.D. Rusk. *Moral Transformation: The Original Christian Paradigm of Salvation.* New Zealand: Bridgehead, 2011.

Wanak, Lee. "Developing an Operational Philosophy of Theological Education: A Primer on Moving from Philosophy to Strategy." In *Foundations for Academic Leadership*, edited by Fritz Deininger and Orbelina Eguizabal, 40–67. Nürnberg, DE: VTR, 2013.

Warfield, B.B. "The Religious Life of Theological Students." *Themelios* 24 (1999) 31–41.

Watkins David A., and John B. Biggs, eds. *The Chinese Learner: Cultural, Psychological, and Contextual Influences.* Hong Kong: Comparative Education Research Centre, 1996.

Williams, Ken. "Toward a Biblical Theology of Suffering." Relationship Skills. http://www.relationshipskills.com/resources/Toward-a-Theology-of-Suffering.pdf.

Wolterstorff, Nicholas. *Justice in Love.* Grand Rapids: Eerdmans, 2011.

Wright, N.T. *Following Jesus: Biblical Reflections on Discipleship.* Grand Rapids: Eerdmans, 1995.

Wytsma, Ken. "Understanding a Theology of Suffering: Sing a New Song." *FaithGateway* (blog). February 3, 2015. https://www.faithgateway.com/understanding-theology-suffering/#.X0fYGpNKhH0.

Yewangoe, Andreas Anangguru. *Theologia Crucis in Asia: Asian Christian Views on Suffering in the Face of Overwhelming Poverty and Multifaceted Religiosity in Asia.* Amsterdam: Rodopi, 1987.